Simplified Husbandship

Simplified Fathership

Simplified Husbandship

Simplified Fathership

Richard M. Eyre

Salt Lake City, Utah

Library of Congress Catalog Card Number: 80:69094
ISBN O-88494-410-7

First Printing, 1980

Lithographed in the United States of America
PUBLISHERS PRESS
Salt Lake City, Utah

Contents

SIMPLIFIED HUSBANDSHIP

To become a better husband —
change yourself
not your wife.

How It Is

1. The Case of the Competing Couple

John loves his wife. This evening he tried to show her so by taking her to dinner. Things didn't go well, and John is worried. It was hard to talk. Two or three times John felt like he was talking to a stranger. The conversation was brittle, stiff. They went home early. John went to work on the things in his briefcase. Mary went to bed wondering vaguely what was wrong but too used to it to feel very upset.

Since John's promotion two years ago, he has had more responsibility, more worries. He has protected Mary from these by not talking about them. Anyway, with two children still in diapers, she has enough to think about. He doesn't ask her much about the children, the house, the bills, since she seems to have them well in hand.

John is finished with his briefcase now. It's late; he's untying his shoes, glancing at his sleeping wife, wondering where the excitement and tenderness of their early marriage has disappeared to. They had a serious fight last week. John had been detained at the office, and Mary and the kids had to go ahead with the special dinner she had planned. When he finally did get home, he wolfed down the carefully re-warmed dinner and exited to the den, saying he had to unwind and watch the late news. Mary caught him off guard by saying she had a little news flash of her own — she was looking for a job. The next three hours were spent in heated argument. She made her case for independence, for fulfillment, for doing meaningful things for people who would appreciate her. He retaliated with a defense of the adequate living he provided, the lack of support he felt from her for his own job, the fact that the kids needed a full-time mother. Fatigue finally ended the argument. John stormed out to the living room and fell asleep on the couch before he could compose his next argument. Mary fumed herself to sleep on the bed. Next morning they were too busy to get back to the point, and they hadn't talked about it since. John had intended to bring it up tonight at dinner, but the right feeling wasn't there. Neither of them was up for another marathon fight so neither brought up the subject.

By the time John is ready for bed, Mary is fast asleep. That night, unlike John, she had not worried more than usual about their relationship. The problems didn't seem new to her. For the past two

years she had been trying to get John to talk about
them, to focus on her worries that they were drawing
apart, that she knew less and less about his world, and
that he cared less and less about hers. His answers
were always not to worry, not to take things so
seriously, not to fret, and besides, he didn't have time
to talk right now.

Mary had felt better since last month, when she'd
decided to get a job. She'd worried about the kids being
with a sitter, but even that was resolved now. It was
time someone started thinking about her — even if that
someone was herself!

2.   The Case of the Flat Marriage

Peter and Shiela walked out of the theater together,
holding hands but not feeling much. It was Saturday
night, their anniversary, and the first time in exactly
a year that they had been out alone together, without
the children.

"The ideal marriage — ten years together without a
fight, with hardly even a cross word." That's what
Peter had said to his mother that afternoon when she
had called to say, "Happy anniversary." He had said
it, and it was true. They never fought; they never
argued. They were as polite to each other as any two
people could be. And they were not unhappy (Peter
was trying to convince himself now). They were defi-
nitely not unhappy.

Peter's mind kept going back to the question he'd heard on the TV quiz show earlier that same afternoon: "How would you describe your marriage — in one word." His own answer kept flashing on and off in his mind: "Flat."

The next day Shiela sat in church, looked at the carpet under the bench in front of her, and tried to ignore the words of the speaker. "The home should be the center of growth, of happiness, of excitement. If your home isn't a happier place now than it was a year ago, you're not progressing. . . ." Shiela couldn't tune out the words. They penetrated because they made her face what she was trying to ignore. She was bored. She was tired. She wasn't sad, but she wasn't happy. She felt stagnant, stuck in neutral, not in pain but somewhat on the edge of it — a little frustrated, a little unfulfilled, a little tired.

But why? She and Peter were on course. They had to be. They were fully active in the Church. They rarely missed a family home evening. She was in the Relief Society presidency; he was in the bishopric. They paid their tithing and lived the Word of Wisdom. She didn't know of any Church program they weren't following or any calling or obligation they weren't keeping. She and Peter never fought. He was almost always pleasant to her. Their friends said they had a model marriage. She was a little disappointed that they hadn't bought that new house yet and a little worried about whether she was communicating very well with the twins, but they certainly weren't failing. So why, she wondered, did she feel she was on a slide — a smooth, fairly comfortable slide where she woke up each day feeling she'd slipped a little lower. Did Peter appreciate the new wallpaper she put in last week? He

said it was "nice," but that was all. And she'd been
trying carefully to get the lawn back in shape, even
mowing it herself last week when the boy didn't come.
But nothing seemed to make Peter really smile these
days.

Peter's thoughts as he sat on the stand during the
same meeting were similar. "I guess I'm just cut out
for the middle. I'm going nowhere fast in my job. I
laugh when I think of all those goals Shiela and I used
to have. Oh well, the kids depend on me. I couldn't
have taken that job offer two months ago anyway.
Small company, too risky, and too far away from
'Zion' and from the folks. At least I'm steady. We
never miss family home evening or temple day. I don't
think Shiela is unhappy. She never complains, anyway. We have good control, the two of us. She's as
good as I am at walking away from something rather
than fighting over it. I guess now is just a time to get
through. Another eight or ten years the kids will be
into college and Shiela and I can start having some fun
together. There'll be more time for the theater then,
and maybe then I can find another job as exciting as
the one I turned down."

3. The Case of the Church-Rival

Preston was whistling when he came in. For the
first time in years, he grabbed Molly around the waist
and swung her off the ground. "You won't believe it,
hun! You may be the wife of the first counselor in the

stake presidency!'' Molly felt her face drop although she tried hard to smile. How could she tell Pres that she'd been hoping the meeting with the stake president was to release him? He had been second counselor for nearly four years. He was a good, devoted man. She was sure he did a good job, that people needed him — but, darn it (the thought forced its way in), *she* needed him, too. She needed *something*. She had never felt so left out, so unimportant, so insignificant.

Before Pres had become so involved in the Church, and while the kids were smaller, it seemed to Molly, they had been the center of her attention and Preston's. She had always loved the homemaker's role, taken pride in her home, her children, her husband, her civic involvement, her Church job. Her life was full. Sometimes hectic and very busy, but full. And it was still full, wasn't it? The kids still needed her and she was still busy with good causes. What was it then? It was Preston. Something more was needed. Why did she relate it to his Church calling? Why did she resent a little the fact that he would probably be in the stake presidency? His time and thoughts would be on that, but surely she could handle it. Surely she was secure enough not to let that bother her.

4. The Case of the Non-communicating Husband

Dwayne simply couldn't believe his eyes. The note was only two lines long: "We've gone. Maybe we can work it out better from a distance. Kate.''

Dwayne looked at the clock. Eleven-fifteen. He'd been working late again. She could have been gone for hours, maybe since morning. Where? Her mother's, probably. Did she get the kids out of school? Why? Had the disagreement been that serious? Was this the separation she'd threatened? Or did she just mean she was leaving for a few days? He'd told her they would talk it out as soon as the pressure was off at the office. Kate usually didn't do hasty things like this — why couldn't she bear with him now? They'd had other problems in their twelve years of marriage and handled them. What was different now? Sure, this time it had gone on longer. They hadn't talked for awhile, but it wasn't that bad, was it?

As Dwayne's mind raced from question to question, Kate was two hundred fifty miles away, her kids tucked into Grandma's bed, her head on her mother's shoulder, her tears making it hard to talk. "Mom, I just don't see how we can work this out. We never talk. He works late more and more. When he's home, he's preoccupied. Our lives are so separate. He doesn't know what the kids are doing or what I'm doing or what I'm feeling or what I'm thinking. And I don't know what he's doing. We haven't talked about his job, I mean really talked, since he changed divisions two years ago. I don't even know how he's doing — or even if he likes his job! The only time we pray together is when it's convenient. The only time we're ever alone together is late when we're both too tired to talk. We never go out except with his clients. He keeps saying we'll get away and really communicate, but it's been two years since we've been away together and that was just a business convention. He was too busy to talk. I *love* him, Mom, but I swear I don't *know* him as well as I did three years ago!"

5.   The Case of the Short Honeymoon

"The honeymoon is really over, isn't it?" Shelly screamed as Bill slammed the door, leaving her alone. Three weeks they had been married, she thought, and reality had just settled in with a bang.

I wonder if I really even know him, Shelly thought. I know I love him, but I don't know if I know him.

The two-week honeymoon had been wonderful—a perfect extension of the courtship. Fun-filled days and tender nights. A few fights, but it was so much fun to make up. Yes, the honeymoon had been perfect. But the week after had been disaster.

First of all, she had discovered that Bill didn't tell her everything. He hid only little things, but they hurt—such as the fact that it was going to take him five quarters instead of three to finish his degree. And that he really couldn't stand the ballet, despite what he'd said earlier. Then there was the car payment bill she'd opened—car payments she didn't know they had. Bill kept saying he didn't want her to worry, that he'd take care of them. She kept saying she was his wife; she wanted to know everything.

The thing that had really set it off, as she thought back, was the second night after they got back. That night Bill had gone out with the boys. "Just for a hamburger," he'd said. "I've still got friends, don't I?" But he hadn't mentioned it until half an hour before they picked him up.

Even that wouldn't have been so bad without what went with it. It seemed silly to worry, but Bill didn't open doors for her anymore or hold her chair. He

didn't even carry her bags when they came back on
the plane.

She had tried to start a talk last Sunday. "Bill,
shall we plan our week? What are we going to do this
month?" Bill had looked at her as if she were his little
sister. "We're going to do what we always do — I'm
going to school and you're going to work. What's to
plan?"

Shelly had cried for a while and then shaken it off.
"Mom told me it wouldn't be all a bed of roses," she
said. "I guess I'd just better buck up and face reality."

6. The Case of the Left-alone Couple

As the station wagon full of grandkids pulled
away, Howard turned and walked back up the steps
and into the quiet house. Madge stayed on the front
walk, waving until the last cloud of dust left by the
departing car had settled.

It seemed that they saw less and less of their three
children and their families. With gas prices still
climbing, weekend visits weren't practical anymore.
Howard wasn't looking forward to the next few days.
He knew the pattern: he and Madge would talk about
the grandkids for the next day or so — what each had
said, how each had grown. They would probably even
laugh a time or two in mutual pride. But that would
pass by tomorrow night, and then the edgy silence
would set in.

For nearly thirty years now, Howard and Madge
had lived for their children. They'd been a happy
family, but it seemed to Howard that, since the last
child had left, things had gone downhill. Sometimes it
seemed he and Madge simply had nothing to talk
about. They were like roommates who had played
together on the football team. Now that football season
was over, they had nothing in common.

7. The Case of the Domineering Wife

"I have to work late. Don't wait up. I'll see you in
the morning." Larry said good-bye and put the phone
back on the hook. He hated to lie to his wife, but if he
went home she would ask him about the job and he
would have to tell her he hadn't even applied for the
assistant principal's position. Maybe by morning
Virginia's offense would not be so potent, and he
would feel stronger in his defense than he did now.

Larry pulled a magazine out of his drawer, propped
his feet up, and tried to pass the time by reading.
Instead, his mind anticipated the exchange they would
have next morning.

He would say, "Ginny, I didn't apply for the job. I
just like teaching more than administration, and I
don't care that much about the status."

She would say, "You don't care about status — you
don't care about anything. You didn't even care about

finishing your degree or moving up from that crummy little school where you first taught. You didn't care about any of them, and you wouldn't have *done* any of them if I hadn't pushed you every step of the way."

He would say, "Ginny, honey . . ."

She would say, "Don't 'Ginny honey' me. Get down there and make that application, or you'll be stuck with those third-graders for the rest of our lives, with a third-grade teacher's salary."

Larry tried again to read the magazine.

At home, Virginia wasn't reading or sleeping. She had guessed the truth. Larry hadn't applied and didn't want to tell her. She knew he thought she was pushing him — he always did. If only Larry would take their lives in hand. Why didn't he plan, why didn't he have a little clearer view of what he wanted from life? The Church taught that the priesthood should lead. Why he didn't even take the lead in getting up on Sunday to go to church? Heaven knows, Virginia thought, I don't like to be the pushy one, but I have to. Otherwise we'd be going nowhere.

8. The Case of the Domineering Husband

They had been on the plane for seven hours before Sue finally got up the courage to mention it. She felt she had to rather than holding it inside for the whole trip. "Harry, I really didn't want to go to Israel, you know. We just have the two weeks, and we really should have visited Pam and the new baby in Toronto.''

Harry didn't get mad. Sue almost wished he would. If he just thought enough of her competence as a person to be mad at her! Instead he gave her that "let me explain it to you again, honey" look and said, "Now, Sue, this is a once-in-a-lifetime thing. We'll see Pam at Christmas.''

It wasn't just the trip, Sue thought. Harry never consulted her on anything, never seemed to think her opinion was even worth asking for. She guessed it had always been that way, but when the kids were at home she had at least had them. When they occupied her time she wasn't as aware of the way he told her to do this rather than asking her, announced decisions to her rather than discussing them. How, when he wanted a deep or spiritual discussion, he looked to his priesthood brethren, never to her.

Suddenly, in a flush of emotion, Sue grabbed Harry's arm and looked him full in the face. "Harry, I'm your wife. We're supposed to be partners. I'm not your maid or your slave.'' She had wanted to say that for years and here it had finally come out, as their plane approached touchdown in London.

Now Harry did get angry, in a quiet, clenched sort of way. "Sue, for heaven's sake, don't make a scene on the airplane. It so happens that we are partners, but I hold the authority and I make the decisions. You take care of the children, and I'll take care of the priesthood. I don't tell you how to keep house, so don't you start telling me how to run our lives!''

How It Ought to Be

A *Family Circle* magazine survey on the attitudes and feelings of wives showed a clear majority (61 percent) who said that the most important thing in marriage was "to have someone close enough to share everything with."

A graphic representation makes the point best. When two spheres come only partly together, or when husband and wife share only part of their lives, the "in-common" portion is shaped like a football.

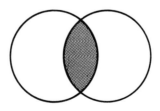

This type of marriage, like a football, is erratic and hard to predict. There is no telling where it will bounce. It can look as though it is coming right to you but then bounce sideways or even backwards.

As a marriage gains oneness, the spheres move together until virtually everything is shared and the common portion is shaped like a basketball.

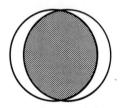

The marriage, like a round ball, becomes predictable and stable. It bounces straight; its course is true.

The best way for a husband to pursue this kind of oneness lies not in efforts to change his wife or even in efforts to change the marriage relationship. His best chance lies in changing himself.

The next section deals with four simple, direct qualities which, when acquired by husbands, can turn a "football" into a "basketball." Each of the four qualities is presented as a "word-peg" — a group of ideas that hang together on a particular word or word-group. Each of the words start with the letter *P*. The qualities are:

    1.   Partnership-plan-pray
    2.   Protect-pamper-'preciate
    3.   Patriarch-priesthood
    4.   Priority

In order to make a difference, these four qualities have to *become part of* a husband, *go into him*, lodge there and stay there. The husband himself has to *change* by taking on these qualities. The final section explains *how* to bring about this change.

Getting from "Is" to "Ought"

1. Partnership-Plan-Pray

Synergism means a situation in which "the whole is greater than the sum of its parts"; wherein two together can do more than two apart. Marriage can be the highest form of synergism, but it takes effort and commitment. Synergism should be the end result of all good partnerships. Good partnerships grow out of 1, communication; 2, complementary roles; 3, shared goals and plans; and 4, inspiration and guidance.

Marriage is a wonderfully natural partnership. It is physically natural in the way man and woman are drawn to each other, comforted and fulfilled by each other, and able to procreate through each other. The marriage partnership is also mentally and emotionally natural as each ego is boosted by the other and as

tender sensitivities complement ambition and aspira-
tions. There is even a spiritual synergism in marriage
which comes through the patriarchal order wherein
a husband and wife share the priesthood and share
eternal covenants and eternal promises that cannot
come to one alone.

Benjamin Franklin understood the synergism of
marriage. He likened a single man to "the odd half of a
pair of scissors."

Let's go back to the four ingredients of a good
partnership.

1. *Communication.* The old adage, "Some
things are better left unsaid," has no place in marriage.
There may be ways in which some things should not
be said, but all things that are *felt*, and as much as
possible of what is thought, *should* be said. Through
the gospel's perspective, we view marriage as an
eternal partnership, even a oneness. *Oneness* is an
impossibility between *two* who share only part of what
they feel. Even disagreements, if they are open and if
love is still felt underneath the conflict, can be helpful.
They usually bring learning and recommittal as they
are resolved.

2. *Complementary roles.* One great fallacy of
certain factions of the Equal Rights movement is an
assumption that *equality* implies *sameness.* Effective
partnerships or teams are almost always built around
"equal but different" roles which complement each
other. In a business, a marketing vice president and a
production vice president do completely different
things of equal importance. On a basketball team, a
guard may set up plays and shoot long jump-shots
while the center concentrates on rebounding and close
in-shots. In an orchestra, the strings may provide the

melody, the percussion section the rhythm. Synergism in marriage springs from two partners finding equality in the roles each is better suited for, rather than trying to make their roles the same.

3.   *Shared goals and plans.* Partnerships become deep and noble as they pursue worthy objectives. Partners become unified and complementary to each other as they work together toward a common goal. Two people may be "pulling the ropes" of two different roles, but those ropes must be tied to the same coach and both must be pulling up the same hill — together, communicating as they go.

4.   *Inspiration.* Just as a three-legged stool is more stable than one with two legs, so a three-way partnership is more reliable. The third partner should be the Lord. Our Heavenly Father stands ready to bless all marriages that desire to become "one." The Holy Ghost is brought into a partnership through prayer. His influence is sufficient to turn a planning session into a vision of potential, and to turn a conflict and impasse into a set of apologies and an agreement based on deeper understanding.

Let's look in on a particular husband (Charles) and his wife (Mary) to see how they went about the process of making their marriage into a true (and synergistic) partnership. You may want to go about it differently, but some of the principles discovered by Charles and Mary will apply equally well to you.

Charles and Mary decided to set up two separate "partnerships" between themselves. One was called the "inside partnership." It dealt with inside-the-home things: the house itself, the children's development, the personal "kingdom" that Charles and Mary were starting now and hoped to continue throughout

eternity. The other was called the "outside partnership." It dealt with outside-the-home things: the
earning of money, the providing of necessities,
involvement in and contributions to worthy "outside
causes" ranging from church to civic. In the inside
partnership, Mary become the general (managing)
partner and Charles the limited (participating) partner.
In the outside partnership, Charles became general
partner, Mary limited partner.

Each night, just before their prayer together, Mary
gives a brief inside partnership "report" to Charles,
and Charles mentions any questions or comments that
he has. Then Charles gives a brief outside partnership
report and Mary responds. Each night becomes a
moment to report to and plan with each other. The
partnership is an equal one. Both partners participate
in both partnerships, but one is in charge of each.

For particularly busy times, during their evening
"partnership meeting" Charles and Mary write out
their individual schedules (where they'll be, what
they'll be trying to do) on a sheet of paper with a carbon
copy underneath. They draw a line down the center
and Charles lists his day on one side, Mary puts hers
on the other. Each has a copy for the next day that
shows what both are doing. When schedules are less
complex, they just discuss each other's upcoming day
before having prayer.

During scheduling, an attempt is made to find an
hour during the coming day when partnership roles
can be reversed. During this hour Charles can be with
the children on the "inside," while Mary shifts to
outside activities, church, civic, or personal.

As Charles and Mary make their partnership
reports and complete "day planning" followed by
evening prayer, they think of the process as a three-

way partnership meeting. Charles is the general
partner in charge of the outside; Mary is the general
partner in charge of the inside; and the Lord, through
the Holy Ghost, is the supervising partner who gives
confirmation to each righteous venture being planned
and prayed about.

The partnership meeting is simple and straight-
forward and seldom takes more than ten minutes. The
results are that:

1. Each learns more about the arena where he or
    she did *not* spend the day (and becomes more
    appreciative of what the other is doing).
2. Each gives input and ideas for the other's
    benefit.
3. Each thinks about what he or she will do the
    next day in both the general and the limited
    role.
4. The prayer becomes far more specific and
    meaningful (because it is *about* things just
    discussed).
5. Both sleep better when the next day is clear
    and challenging rather than hazy and un-
    certain.

Charles and Mary expand their partnership
meeting a little on Sunday and look at the whole week
together. They decide what the objectives of the
"inside" and "outside" should be for that week, go
over their schedules, and see that no appointment or
commitment is overlooked. They end these sessions
with a simple, private, two-way testimony meeting.
They find that, in a spirit of testimony, all feelings are
expressed clearly — both love and worries, anticipation
and concern.

Toward the end of each month, Charles and Mary arrange to go out together for dinner. They spend that one evening viewing their partnerships from a monthly perspective. Mary uses a particular format for her "inside" report. It consists of thinking of each child in terms of how he is doing physically, mentally, emotionally, socially, and spiritually. Charles contributes his thoughts, and both gain insight into each of their children. Charles then leads a discussion of "outside" matters ranging from what he is doing at work to family finances. Together, Charles and Mary set some simple monthly goals both "inside" and "outside."

They also make a point of taking a short "honeymoon" vacation once a year in the winter. During this trip they discuss their partnership for the *year* past and the *year* ahead.

Charles and Mary's three-way partnership works well for them. There are many ways of getting the same result. Your method may be different, but the principles involved should be the same:

1. Total communication or openness.
2. Complementary roles (separate but shared responsibility).
3. Shared goals and plans.
4. Adding the Lord to your partnership through earnest, regular prayer together.

If exaltation is the goal, marriage partnerships must fold together in purpose and communication until they become *one*. We often imagine that temple marriages differ from civil marriages in *quantity* (they last longer), but, in fact, their quantity will be great

only if their *quality* is great, only if oneness is obtained.
Oneness means exactly what it implies — being able
to feel what the other feels, reason with each other's
logic.

Oneness means much more than "getting along,"
merely being conciliatory. "Agreeing to disagree" on
some things is fine among friends and business
partners but not between marriage partners striving
for oneness. A great marriage partnership may not be
in constant agreement on everything, but partners
will communicate (in the three-way mode) until they
do come together. It is not oneness when one gives in
to the other, accepts the other's wishes against his
own, "goes along with" the other. A oneness partnership requires enough communication to get to the
same point together. This principle is well illustrated
by the physical dimension of marriage. It is better for
one partner to "bridle" his passions and wait until they
are *matched* than for the other partner to "give in"
or "go along with." The same principle should be
applied to mental, emotional, even spiritual unity.

As husbands, we can work toward oneness
through patience, by creating understanding and
communication rather than competition. Partners are
separated when they compete in any context other
than fun.

Emerson said, "Marriages do not fail, people fail.
All marriages do is show those failures up." As
husbands, we should guard against our own failures
to communicate, to plan together with our wives, and
to pray together. In short, we should form a "oneness"
partnership where all things are shared. As we do
this, the meaning of the Savior's words will gradually
become clear: "The kingdom of God is within you."
(Luke 17:21.)

The Word-peg "Partnership-Plan-Pray"—a Summary

A husband who is "self-programming" the concept of "partnership-plan-pray" says to himself:

- ▶ My wife is my partner in all I do.
- ▶ We share everything, including our deepest feelings.
- ▶ We plan our time together and share objectives for our lives inside and outside our home.
- ▶ We pray together regularly, and preceding the prayer is a discussion of our partnership.

2. Protect-Pamper-'Preciate

My mind will never forget the vision of true chivalry that my teenage eyes once observed. I was standing by the Salt Lake tabernacle at conference time when President McKay's car pulled up. The driver helped the ninety-year-old prophet out and then helped him inch his way to the other car door so that *he* could help his wife out. He opened Emma's door and took her hand. I watched her smile as she stood to walk with him.

It is not unnatural for a man to help his wife, to treat her with deference, to protect and pamper her. It is not old-fashioned, nor patronizing, nor condescending. It is natural and right. It gives a woman a

kind of warm, cherished feeling that awakens in her
the strengths of support, loyalty, and oneness with
her husband.

I'll also remember a day in the late sixties. I was a
student at Harvard University's business school, and
we had in our class two women who were particularly
strident representatives of the newly popularized
movement called Women's Liberation. Some problem
in our case study that day so offended them that they
took the floor and let fly a heated verbal assault on
the chauvinists of the world and on how tired they
were of being patronized and treated as though they
were any different from men.

Seated next to me was a Frenchman named
Dominique, very Latin and very strong-willed. I
watched the color rise in his cheeks until he could take
no more. He stood up, swept to the front of the class
and defended manhood and chivalry. "All that is
wrong with you two," he boomed, "is that you have
never met a real man. You've never found anyone
strong enough to make you glad you are women. You
don't know that a man and woman together, who love
each other, can be a team." He said he didn't defend
those who felt women were of less worth than men.
He said that he felt women were of *more* worth than
men, and thus he treated them with respect and
chivalry.

Every marriage counselor has heard it a thousand
times. The wife says, "There's no romance in our
marriage anymore. He never compliments me, never
surprises me, never *courts* me anymore." The husband
says, "She doesn't take care of herself as she used to.

She's lost that certain appeal. She doesn't make me
feel the way I used to."

Each thinks he or she can't change until the other
one does. In fact, either could change the other simply
by changing himself. The wife could likely change the
husband by making herself more appealing—but this
is a book to husbands. Just as the man initiates much
of the courtship before marriage, he should take the
initiative after marriage.

What we are talking about here, in essence, is ego.
A woman's ego is no weaker than a man's, but hers
works in a slightly different way. Hers usually is best
fed when she is cared for, complimented, appreciated,
protected—even pampered a bit—not with the
patronizing implication that she is weaker, less able,
but with the implication that she is *more* special,
important, and genuinely valued. A wife who receives
sincere compliments, who is appreciated, who feels
needed and cherished and protected, seems to gain a
soft strength, a kind of clear-headed fulfillment that
raises her toward her full potential in many areas.

It's the old notion of "out-giving" that can make
marriages even more beautiful. Have you ever watched
what happens to a basketball team when one player
is so unselfish that he is always looking for a team-
mate to get the ball to? Other players respond in kind.
The ball moves faster; everyone gets better shots. The
teamwork of marriage can be similar. A husband who
tries to please his wife by being chivalrous, by
making her feel protected and cherished, will find that
his wife tries to please him in how she looks, how she
supports him—little things she does for him. It is one
very clear application of the Savior's admonition-

promise: Cast your bread upon the waters and it will return to you again.

We all remember (even in our dreams) the dizzy beauty of falling in love, the romance, the six-inches-off-the-ground feeling of being swept away with love. Most of us, however, assume that this must be a short-term condition that slides away as the realities of marriage and family set in. Actually, it is not the *addition* of responsibility and children that destroy romance. It is the *subtraction* of courtship, of chivalry, of living to make the other person happy.

One of the most direct ways for a husband to continue his courtship is to take his wife out on dates. Just as valid as reserving one night per week to be together as a family, is the practice of reserving one night to go out together as husband and wife. It becomes a time to focus on each other, to enjoy the things about each other that first caused you to fall in love. The dates should be as planned or as spontaneous, as elaborate or as simple, as elegant or as casual as were your dates during your pre-marriage courtship.

The Word-peg "Protect, Pamper, 'Preciate" — a Summary

A husband who is practicing the concept of "protect, pamper, 'preciate" says to himself:

► I love my wife deeply and understand her
need to feel cherished and loved.

► I feel tenderness toward her and want to
find meaningful ways to compliment her,
to be chivalrous and protective of her.

► I watch her closely and notice the times
she needs the "lift" of a tender kiss, a
word of sincere appreciation, a helping
hand, a date.

3.   Patriarch-Priesthood

Many years ago, during our courtship, Linda and
I went to a particular Church leader to ask for his
advice regarding our marriage. He knew us both
rather well and perceived that we each had stiff necks
and strong wills. His advice took an unexpected tack.

He moved his chair closer to Linda, looked her in
the eye, and asked, "What would you do if Richard
were to ask you to do something you didn't agree with,
not something unrighteous, but something you didn't
want to do?"

Linda's response was thoughtful. "I would tell
him I didn't want to, and we would discuss it."

"Yes, and most things you would work out and
agree on. But let's say in this instance you still didn't
agree. You thought it was the wrong decision, but he
still wanted it. What would you do?"

Now Linda's eyes were flashing a bit and her
response was predictable. "I wouldn't do it."

Our advisor leaned back in his chair, "That's what
I want to talk to you about," he said. "You would
have two options in that situation. One, to refuse. Or
two, to say, 'Yes, you know my feelings, but if you still
feel it is right, I will accept your decision.' If you take
the first option you get into a power struggle and
minimize his chance to change or repent if he is
wrong (his ego, if you defy him, will lock him into his
wrong choice). If you take the second option, you show
trust and giving, and you *maximize* his chance to
change if his decision is wrong. (The other side of the
husband's ego is the one which feels the responsibility
to protect and be fair with the wife who puts her
confidence in him.)

Our advisor then left Linda to think about what he
had said and turned to me. (I had enjoyed their inter-
change and was happy to be a spectator but, as it
turned out, his most pointed message was to me.) He
said, "Would you ever do that?"

I said, "Do what?"

He said, "Demand that your wife do something
she did not agree with?"

I guess I thought about it too long, because, before
I could answer, he went on. "If you do, you will sooner
or later destroy your relationship. If you force decisions
on her, you abuse her trust and become a tyrant.
That is what you do if you demand."

He paused and let us both think for a moment,
then smiled, lightened his tone a little, and sum-
marized. "If *either* of you remember what I've said,
it will work. If Linda respects the priesthood, you will
use it well. If you counsel and communicate rather

than demand, she will respect you and you will be one,
with the priesthood belonging to both of you together."

As husbands, we must realize that wives want our
leadership as well as our partnership—not "master-
slave" leadership, not "greater-leading-lesser" leadership, but *priesthood* leadership—prayerful, gentle, but
strong. No woman wants weakness in her husband.
The stronger a woman is, the more she wants strength
in her husband. The most secure, personally strongest
women I know are not the ones who lead their
husbands, but the ones who follow their husbands in
a partnership-priesthood sense of the word.

In a baseball game the pitcher throws the ball, the
catcher catches it. The roles are equal but different.
They could rotate, the catcher throwing every other
pitch, but they would do less well in the game. In the
patriarchal order, the husband holds the priesthood
and the wife shares it. The "head of the home" (the
husband's role) and the "heart of the home" (the wife's
role) are equal but different in that both draw on the
great, inherent strengths of each.

The beauty, the romance, and much of the
excitement of life lies in the inherent differences
between men and women. The differences, if respected,
can bring about security, fulfillment, joy, and can
help form an eternal bond. Ignoring or denying the
differences leads to competition, jealousy, insecurity,
and family separation.

A close friend of mine was worried about his
marriage and decided that rather than seeking to
change his wife he should go to work on himself. He
determined to win greater respect from his wife by

being a better priesthood leader. His plan was a simple one. It included only four things:

1. Take the lead in planning their week together each Sunday.
2. Use the priesthood more in the home (for blessings, etc.).
3. Have a short personal interview with each child on Sunday evening.
4. Hold a good family prayer each morning and a "partnership prayer" with his wife each night.

The effects were almost immediate. He began to think about his wife's needs as he sat with her to plan. His mind focused more on where they were going as a family and what things he could do for each child. But the most noticeable change was in his wife. The nagging ceased; there was no more implied criticism about his career or his inconsistent child discipline. It seemed to him that she was suddenly more interested in him, more tender to him, more supportive of him. It turned out that she, like so many wives, wanted more than anything to have a priesthood leader in the home — one she could respect, look up to, follow, one she could communicate with, one she could encourage to reach toward his very best.

Another husband I am aware of sat down one night and drafted two lists. One was titled, "What I must be to her." The other was headed, "What she needs." The first list included things such as:

1. A strong leader.
2. A tender sympathizer.
3. An active partner in the home and with the children.

The list of needs included:

1. Someone very strong to believe in, to be devoted to, to give herself to.
2. Fuller confidence in her own abilities to contribute and to succeed.
3. The warm feeling of being completely needed, appreciated, cherished.

The Word-peg "Patriarch-Priesthood" — a Summary

A husband who is programming the concept of "patriarch-priesthood" says to himself:

► My wife shares the priesthood with me, and we are equal partners. But I *hold* that authority and I have the righteous strength that helps her feel secure and fulfilled in her support.

► I take the lead in planning and goal-setting, in family prayer, and in personal interviews with each of the children.

► I realize that there is no intervening link in the priesthood chain between myself and the Lord. As a father I am entitled to direct inspiration for my wife and children. I ask for that inspiration and receive it.

► I *use* the priesthood often in my home for personal blessings and to keep the Lord's Spirit present.

4.   Priority

Marriage is too important and too demanding to allow success to one who views it simply as a way to meet his needs or as a casual arrangement requiring less concern or attention than his job or his church calling.

Successful marriage demands from every husband *commitment*, first to the eternal responsibility of the marriage itself, second to his wife as his highest priority.

The essential meaning of marriage, in its civil as well as eternal form, is *commitment*. If commitment between marriage partners is not genuine and total, they are merely living together. Lack of commitment is Satan's key tool in destroying relationships. Without commitment, little problems and disagreements can become *final* ones.

The point of this chapter is that a husband's commitment to stay married is not enough. Devotion to his wife must be part of his commitment and his highest priority.

An interesting (often worrisome) exercise is to make a list of your highest priorities, and then a second list, of where you actually put the most thought and energy. The first list, for many of us, would look something like this:

1.   Wife
2.   Children
3.   Church calling
4.   Job

The second, if we are honest, often looks like this:

1.   Job

2. Church calling
3. Children
4. Wife

Many of us fall into the trap of rationalizing-reasoning. We say, "My wife is pretty self-sufficient; she doesn't need much of my time. We're both busy, and she understands. We have faith in each other. She'd rather have me do well at work than worry about her all the time. We're each working on our kids and our other jobs, not on each other."

The problem with this thinking is that it robs us of the unique beauty a marriage can have — the beauty of knowing that someone else puts you first, of trying to out-give someone who is trying to out-give you. The magic of marriage is that, when two people give each other first priority, each becomes more confident, more capable of succeeding in all *other* priorities. A wife who feels secure that her husband thinks of her first, becomes herself a better mother, a better leader, and better at all her other roles, including her role as wife.

I have two particular friends who I have always felt were especially good husbands, remarkably aware of their wives' needs. Both Steve and Boyd seem to me to be still very much in love with their wives. I asked both of them the same question. "How do you manage, as busy as you are, to do so many things for your wife, to be so considerate of her?" Their answers were rather different, but, as I think about it, both added up to essentially the same thing.

Steve, an organized, systematic type of guy, gave this response: "In addition to planning *with* my wife, I consciously 'prioritize' my wife in my personal planning. When I plan my week, I think about her first, and the first thing I put on my calendar is our Friday night date. Then I ask her about her schedule and try to work out when she might need me. I try to plan at least one little surprise for her each week.''

Boyd, less of a planning type, applied the same principles but in a different way. He said: ''I just watch Patti and try to notice when she needs a little pick up. Also, and I don't always remember this, I try to make my last thought of the day, just before I go to sleep, be of Patti. I think, 'What can I do for Patti tomorrow?' It's amazing. An answer usually is obvious. Most often they're just little things — call her from work, run some errands. Sometimes I just decide I'll bring her a flower or a bag of cashew nuts or any little thing that comes to mind. It's fun to try to think of her for a moment each night just as I doze off. I even think I sleep better when I do.''

Now, it's interesting: I know Patti and I have seen how many little things she does for Boyd, how she ''first prioritizes'' him. I don't know who started it, but I know it works both ways. It's the same with Steve and his wife.

I once gave a talk to a group of young married couples in which I used a pane of one-way glass. In one light the pane was a mirror. In stronger light, it became a window. The message was that when we have the Light of Christ, we view life as a window through which we can see other people and respond to their needs. Without the Light, our lives are mirrors wherein we see only ourselves and do things for others only when there is ''something in it for us.'' On the way home from the speech, I decided that I ought to *apply* the principle as well as talk about it. Since then

I have tried to think of at least two or three conscious "window deeds" to do for Linda every week. Like Boyd's, my "deeds" are often fairly simple — maybe a little poem or changing the tap washer — but they mean something to her. I also know that thinking of "window deeds" helps me think about Linda and be more conscious of her as my first priority. Some caution should be expressed here. One of the "deeds" (washing the Sunday dishes) was so well received that it became a permanent responsibility.

As nice as "window deeds," poems, flowers, and little presents are, they do not, by themselves, constitute the principle of *priority.*

Really putting one's wife first includes some deeper things. It includes a deep inner decision that her needs really are your chief concern. It includes making some conscious sacrifices for her, perhaps some trade-offs that favor her over other important interests.

Some of these trade-offs may be major, such as choosing the job that lets her live where she can pursue her music interests. Some may be small, such as missing the company party so you can take her to her favorite restaurant on her birthday.

I remember a small incident that still means a lot to Linda. We had planned a special evening. But, just as I was leaving the office, I got a call inviting me to a reception for the former President of the United States. I declined, and the evening turned out to be even more special than we'd planned.

In the scriptures, Paul admonishes husbands to "love their wives even as their own bodies." I think it is his way of saying we should not only *care* for our wives more than for ourselves, but *think* about their personal needs as much as we think about our own.

I admire the statement a man once made about his
wife: "She is not only my wife, my sweetheart, my
partner, and the mother of my children, she is my best
friend." The purest definition of "friend" is "one
about whom we deeply care."

Real love is selfless love. Christ's love focused on
others' needs, never on His own. This "pure love of
Christ" is called "charity" in the Book of Mormon.

The bond that husbands should seek with their
wives could be called "charitable friendship" —
thinking more of her than of self.

The Word-peg "Priority" —a Summary

A husband who is practicing the concept of
"priority" says to himself:

- ► My wife comes first in my plans, my
schedule, my priorities.
- ► When I have decisions to make, my first
thought is always how they will affect her.
- ► I consciously try to find "little things" to
do for her on a regular basis.

Turning Outer Theory into Inner Reality

Understanding something and *becoming* something are two different things. If you have read the preceding section carefully, you probably understand the four principles it mentions. The trick is absorbing those principles.

A husband who understands the four principles can apply them when he is conscious of them, but a husband who *becomes* those qualities can apply them *subconsciously*, when he is not thinking about them. Most husbands, busy with jobs, callings, and concerns of all varieties, cannot be constantly thinking of their roles as husbands. Therefore, *becoming* these four qualities to the point where you live them naturally is the only practical, workable way to improve your husbandship.

The question is how?

The answer lies in the amazing capacity of the subconscious mind to be *programmed.* We can actually "feed in" to our subconscious minds the precise qualities of "husbandship" that we would like to have, and, if we are consistent and repetitive enough in that feeding process, we will *become* these qualities.

What is needed is a simple, repetitive *method* of programming the subconscious. The programming itself is very basic and involves only two things:

1.   Being so familiar with the four principles that each becomes a "word-peg." Thus, when you repeat in your mind "partnership-plan-pray," the whole concept of that quality enters your mind, all hanging on the word-peg. Reading back through each of the four principles a few times will make you familiar enough with them that this will happen.

2.   Having a routine of repeating the four word-pegs in your mind until they become a subsconscious part of you. In repeating them, you use the positive approach, saying to yourself: "My wife is my *partner*; we *plan* everything together, *pray* about everything together." While saying this, you are thinking of recent moments when you and your wife have planned and prayed together, thus reinforcing your commitment to the principle. There also come to mind the times you failed to plan, pray, or include your wife, and you resolve to do better. Then you go on to the second principle: "I *protect* my wife, *pamper* her, *'preciate* her." You are thinking of when you had her take a rest the night before while you put the kids to bed, how you thanked her for last night's dinner, etc. You also remember things you overlooked, and you determine how to do better.

The mind is fast. Once you are familiar with what each of the four word-pegs really means, your mind can think of it, analyze how well you're doing on it, and commit you to do better—all in only a few moments.

There are at least four good, regular, and rather enjoyable ways to do this self-programming. Whichever method you choose, you should do it every day until the principles become part of you and then at least two or three times a week from then on. I happen to prefer the first method, but one of the others may be best for you.

Method 1 - running. Go running (or swimming) regularly. While you are running, repeat in your mind each of the four word-pegs, thinking about each in the way just explained. Again, use the word-pegs to *describe* yourself (i.e., "I put my wife first," etc.).

I like the running method because I am helping my body while I program my mind. Vigorous exercise somehow opens up the subconscious mind and makes it more susceptible to being programmed. Thaddens Kostrubala, author of *The Joy of Running*, says running is "a new and powerful way of reaching the unconscious."

Method 2 - meditation. The same kind of self-programming can be done in meditation. Simply sit comfortably in a quiet place, close your eyes and quiet your mind as best you can. Then begin— "I put my wife first," etc.

Method 3 - in the morning while shaving. The nice thing about shaving is that it's regular and predictable. We each do it every day, usually at the same place and at about the same time. One can get

into the habit of self-programming while shaving. The
same mental pattern applies: "I think of my wife as a
partner," etc.

Method 4 - the last thought of the day. People who
don't fall asleep the moment their head hits the pillow
can self-program as they go to bed each night. The
quiet night, with no light or distraction, is a good
time to say, "I am the *patriarch* of my home. I lead
righteously through the *priesthood*. Last week I gave a
priesthood blessing to little Nell. I watch for opportunities to use the priesthood." And so on.

Whichever of the four methods you use (or if you
devise a fifth method of your own), the basic concept
is the same. Describe yourself, using the four word-
pegs. Recall to mind all the "evidence" you can that
you *are* these qualities. Think ahead to future
opportunities to *be* them. Commit yourself.

As you do this regularly, the principles will expand
in your subconscious. They will become as much a
part of you as your name, and you will begin to live
them subconsciously, naturally, consistently, spontaneously — without consciously trying.

Each method of self-programming can be
strengthened by prayer. We have great power to
change ourselves, but our Heavenly Father is the true
changing force. We should ask Him, in our deepest,
personal prayers, to *help* us in the development of
these qualities of better husbandship.

Eight Cases Revisited

The wives in the eight case studies that opened the book may have their problems, but for our purposes the husbands are the culprits. Let's take a brief glimpse at what the four concepts of simplified husbandship could do for each of them. If you really want to see how the concepts apply, reread the eight cases after becoming familiar with the four qualities.

1. The Competing Couple

As John self-programs "*partnership-plan-pray*," he will understand Mary better and she will understand him. They will help each other and share responsibilities as well as feelings. As John self-programs *"priority,"* he will make Mary feel more important than his job and more needed in support of things he is doing in the world.

2.   The Flat Marriage

As Peter self-programs *"protect-pamper-'preciate,"* he will put romance back into his relationship with Shiela. As he programs *"patriarch-priesthood,"* he will lead with more strength and succeed more in Shiela's eyes. They will become more romantic and exciting as a couple and as a family.

3.   The Church-Rival

As Preston self-programs *"priority,"* Molly will feel more needed, more secure, and more inclined to support Pres in his calling rather than resent it.

4. The Non-communicating Husband

As Dwayne self-programs "*partnership-plan-pray*," he can rejuvenate his marriage. All Kate really needs is to feel that she is sharing his life, his successes and his failures.

5. The Short Honeymoon

As Bill self-programs "*priority*," Shelly will realize that she is more important than "the boys." As he works on "*protect-pamper-'preciate*," she will know the honeymoon is not over. And as he programs "*patriarch-priesthood*" and "*partnership-plan-pray*," she will look to him as head of her new home and feel the excitement of sharing his life. (Bill, just starting, ought to work hard on all four qualities.)

6. The Left-alone Couple

As Howard applies "*protect-pamper-'preciate*," Madge will feel the old romance return that was there the "other time" they were without children — during courtship. As Howard self-programs *"partnership-plan-pray,"* they will become more reliant on each other, more excited about doing things together, and less sorrowful about being separated from their grown children.

7.   The Domineering Wife

As Larry programs *"patriarch-priesthood,"* Virginia will use her strength to support him rather than to undermine him or badger him.

8.   The Domineering Husband

Harry really needs to self-program all four qualities, particularly *"priority"* and *"partnership-plan-pray,"* until he and Sue develop a real marriage, something they have obviously not had to this point.

SIMPLIFIED FATHERSHIP

To become a better father —
change yourself
not your children.

Why Is Fathership So Difficult and So Important?

Let's get straight to the point: Fathership is not easy! Most of us fathers, in our candid moments, acknowledge two problems:

1. We *know* we're not doing as well as we should.
2. We *don't know* just how to improve.

The reason our shortcomings as fathers bother us so much is simple: We know, more than any other fathers of any other age, how important our fathership role is—

1. to our children's present happiness;
2. to *our* present happiness;
3. to our children's future;
4. to our future;
5. to society's future;

6. to our children's eternity;
7. to our eternity.

Fathership is, in the eternal context of the gospel, vastly important. It is a key to much of what lies ahead. Until this life, fathership was God's role, His only. When we came to this earth, we made the greatest of eternity's transitions, assuming the fathership role ourselves— we hope to keep it for eternity. There is no greater stewardship, no greater source of potential joy or of potential sorrow.

Let's get straight back to the point: Fathership is not easy! It is life's greatest challenge. Fathership is hard because we've never done it before. It's hard because we're dealing with the most complex things on earth: new human lives. It's hard because the only being in the universe who really knows how is our Heavenly Father.

Now, stop for a moment. It's hard because God is the only one who knows how. But that is also the reason *we* can do it, and do *well* at it— because our Heavenly Father will *help* us (individually, personally) to be good fathers, *if* we ask, *if* we try, *if* we make it a high enough priority.

Fathership is also hard because we get so much advice, and because so much of that advice is *bad* advice. There are so many books on parenthood, so many schools of technique.

Many of these techniques work *against* us. They give us things we are too busy to think about and to do. They tell us to *program* our *time*, and our time won't program. They obscure the natural impulses of loving fathership by filling our minds with what to say and how, where, and when to say it.

The assumption I make here is that you are a father by *inheritance* and by *nature*, that you can do the right thing even when you don't know the right thing — because fathership is *in* you. This section of the book suggests how to get it *out*.

Let's get back once again to the point. Fathership isn't easy, but it *is* natural. You do have fathership inside of you. It was bred there through the premortal eternities. It was taught by the perfect example of the only Father there. It is in us.

The key to fathership does *not* lie outside us, in our children, or in what we say and do to them. It lies within us, in what *we* really are, in what we find inside and build inside. Becoming a great father is an inner process. The starting point is within — with what we really *are*. When we start there, we change ourselves. Then, almost without effort, we change our children. We build them, lift them, and keep them forever as part of our eternal kingdom.

Certain *truths* about fathership and families are self-evident and unchangeable. Let's review some of them.

1. *Families are heavy, profound, eternal responsibilities.*
    "'Teach . . . truth and soberness . . . to love . . . and to serve . . .'" (Mosiah 4:15.)

Bring them up in the nurture and admonition
of the Lord." (Ephesians 6:4.)

"Train up a child in the way he should go: and
when he is old, he will not depart from it."
(Proverbs 22:6.)

". . . Inasmuch as parents . . . teach them not,
. . . the sin be upon the heads of the parents."
(D&C 68:25.)

2. *Families are the foundation of civilization.*

Every society that has flourished has been firmly
founded upon strong families and homes. The early
success of the American democracy can be attributed
to the family. There was little social progress in the
first 250 years following Columbus's landing. Most
"Americans" were French and Spanish seekers of
fortune, more oriented to the pursuit of wealth than to
serious settlement. America, like the Orient and all
great civilizations of progress and stability, became
great with the arrival of strong families who wanted to
build real homes.

Without strong fathers, there cannot be strong
families.

3. *Families are the cradle of this life's happiness
and of eternity's greatest joy.*

The great statement by President David O. McKay,
"No other success can compensate for failure in the
home," has an equally true counterpart: "No other
achievement can provide great enough happiness to
compensate for lack of happiness in the home."

The fact is that happiness is connected more to
things of the family than to any other variable. We
often pity those who have fewer material things or who
live in less developed societies. In truth, though,

happiness is related chiefly to *relationships*, particularly *family relationships*, which are not limited by lack of wealth or modernization. The aborigine of the Australian bushland, if he has a loving, unified family, and if he fills his role of *father* as best he can, will experience more joy and happiness than the most successful man in the most sophisticated society who does not have a happy home.

As mentioned earlier, there is a seemingly infinite quantity and variety of current books on child-rearing and on husband-wife relationships. They are filled with ideas, systems, techniques, and approaches. They offer solutions for every imaginable problem.

There are only two drawbacks. First, few people have (or take) the time to *read* them. Second, few have (or develop) the time or the discipline required to *implement* them. Every time I start reading one, I find myself thinking: "This is a great idea, and so is this, and so is this. If I just didn't have to work, if I didn't have a Church job, if I could devote all of next year to it, I think I could make it work!"

The general fallacy of many child-rearing books is that they advocate what could be called "time programming." They tell us *what* we should do, explain to us *how* to do it, and encourage us to program our time in such a way that we *will* do it. There is certainly some merit in this. But let's be blunt. What *happens* normally is something like this:

Dad knows that Jimmy needs more confidence in himself, so he decides to use the technique of building a model plane with him, "one on one," and praising Jimmy for how well he does on it. Dad decides he'll do it Thursday evening. But his home teaching

companion calls and they go out Thursday night.
Dad resets the model-building time for next Wednes-
day. But there are problems at the office so he doesn't
make it. He plans it again for next Tuesday. But
Tuesday is such a tough day at work that he is too
exhausted when he comes home. The next time he
schedules it, another child has a problem so Dad
postpones the model again. Finally, a month or so
later, he *does* get home early and he *does* take Jimmy
into his room to start the model. But Jimmy doesn't
want to right now. "Could we do it another night,
Dad? My favorite TV show's on now."

The problem with father programming his *time* (to
help a child or to improve an aspect of their relationship) is two-fold:

1.   Time is very hard to program.
2.   Children are very hard to program.

The time will slip away. Then, when you have the
time, *they* may not have the inclination.

*The theory of "Simplified Fathership" is that
usually the father is programming the wrong thing.
What he should be programming is his own mind.
He should be internally developing the qualities of
fathership that will cause him to respond properly to
needs and situations at the moment they arise
rather than at the times he "programs" them to
happen.*

In other words, you become a better father by
changing *yourself*— not by changing your child.

This book suggests a short list of qualities which,
when internalized, will improve a person's perfor-

mance as a father *whenever* (at *each* moment) he is
involved with his children. These qualities are defined
and made clear in terms of their application to the
wide variety of situations and circumstances that a
father faces. As he *becomes* the person with these
qualities, he no longer has to worry so much about
programming his time. Rather, he will find that he is
reacting as he should *whenever* the opportunity arises.
He will give Jimmy confidence *when* Jimmy needs it
—when the "teaching moment" arises—and he will
do it automatically, without planning, without the
scheming that gets in the way of spontaneity and the
simple expression of natural love. Many techniques
are mentioned herein, but they are only there to
illustrate the principles or qualities. A reader's effort
should not be to copy the examples, but rather to
understand the qualities and make them a part of him.
Most of the examples, in fact, were not planned but
came to mind spontaneously to fathers who were
simply striving to *have*, within them, certain qualities
of fathership.

What Four Qualities Simplify Fathership?

As a missionary several years ago on Long Island, I lived with a family that seemed to me to be desperately unhappy. We were teaching several families at that time, and each of them also seemed predominantly unhappy. I wanted to discern the common factors that made them all unhappy. Were there patterns that predicted unhappiness? I couldn't find any failings common to all the families. The unhappiness in each seemed to have its own unique character and causes. There appeared to be so *many* ways to fail that no family had to borrow a method from any other.

Then one day we met a truly happy family. I felt instantly at home in their home. Things they did reminded me of things my family did at home; *they* reminded me of my family. Here was a different background, different beliefs, a wholly different environment, yet it was somehow the same. The faces, the looks, the touches, the feelings were somehow exactly the same as in my own happy home.

By coincidence, I read something not long afterward that explained the experience. Leo Tolstoy said: "Happy families are all alike; every unhappy family is unhappy in its own way."

There *are* some common qualities in all happy homes. They are found in all happy homes because they are the ingredients of happy families. A major part of these required "ingredients" are the four qualities defined in "Simplified Fathership." They are the responsibilities of the patriarch — the father. But how does a father *find* them, *get* them, *keep* them, and *use* them?

The qualities number only four. They will not mean much the first time they are read, but as they are explained and expanded to their full meaning, we will see that they are the essence of good fathership. They are the key to simplified fathership.

The qualities are:
1.   Confidence
2.   Consultantship
3.   Calmness-Consistency-Congruence
4.   Concentration

Each of these words becomes a "peg" on which several related concepts can hang. By reading the discussion carefully, *you* will turn each of the four terms into an image of fathership in your mind. As you mentally repeat that word, it will "program" you so that, *whenever* a situation calls for that particular quality, you will respond *automatically*.

For example, the first word-concept is *confidence*. Elaborated in this chapter is the child's need for self-confidence and for feeling the father's confidence. The factors that contribute to or undermine confidence are explored. Examples of small moment-to-moment ways of showing confidence are illustrated (from tone of voice to recognizing a child's unique gifts). The overall concept is "packaged" into the word *confidence*.

The heart of "Simplified Fathership" is that these principles can be internalized or "programmed" into the consciousness (and subconsciousness) of a father by a self-programming technique. We will draw on the findings of clinical psychologists to present a method of word-identification, or repetitive thought-processing, that can help a father change his *image* of his fathership until his actual *ability* is increased. Essentially, the method involves repeating the word-pegs (and calling to mind the attached concepts of each) at particular times of the day when the mind would otherwise be idle. The word-pegs are mentally rehearsed as though they were already self-descriptive; e.g., "I have a quality of *calmness* when I am around my children."

1.   Confidence

I once observed a local basketball team which was high on talent yet low on victories. The coach criticized, threatened, demanded, became exasperated, got angry, placed blame, changed strategy, and yelled. The players became tense, made more mistakes, lost confidence, and lost ball games.

The next year I watched the same players with a new coach. He encouraged, praised, assumed players knew without being told when they made mistakes, applauded, congratulated, agonized with, helped. The team loosened up, improved, had fun, gained confidence, and won ball games.

People respond to confidence. People live up to the images they perceive others have of them. Especially little people. The sensitivities of children are remarkable. They sense displeasure, anger, or lack of confidence even when an adult thinks he is concealing it or even when an adult is not aware of his feelings himself.

Our daughter was having a hard time with piano lessons. We wondered why they were so hard for her. She knew we wondered. She got slower. One day I praised her for how straight and gracefully she sat on the piano stool. That day she had her best practice. The next day I told her how long and lovely her fingers were on the keyboard. She did better. I told her so. She sensed that I meant it. She did better still.

When I taught our oldest daughter to ski, I tried to be technical. "Bend more at the knee. No, feel the front of your boots with your legs. Careful, don't catch that edge. Wait, now — is that how I said to hold your poles?" The second weekend she said she'd decided she really didn't want to ski. We persevered, but she made slow progress. The next year I taught the second

daughter. "That's super—how did you know how to
buckle that boot? Good snowplow! You're a natural at
this. Hey, are you sure you haven't been having secret
lessons?" I was careful not to give compliments I
didn't mean. I looked for aspects she *did* do well. I
found them. I was pleased. She knew it. After one day
she was better than her sister had been after a full
season. I tried the same confidence retroactively on the
older daughter. It worked.

One day our son did a rare thing—he cleaned his
room. The lavish praise I dished out got that room
cleaned every day for the next two weeks.

All children have unique gifts. A parent who can
recognize them will magnify them. He will feel real
confidence in the child which the child will sense in a
hundred subtle ways. Strength leads to strength.
Confidence grows.

Criticism (by word, look, tone, or even vibration)
hurts the delicate ego of small children. They become
discouraged or rebellious or confused.

Beyond food, shelter, and sleep, a child's greatest
need is attention. Attention comes in two forms:
positive and negative. To a child, *either* is better than
none. A child otherwise ignored will repeat negative
behavior again and again for the *attention* of punishment. If the negative attention he gets for hitting his
baby sister is more substantial than the praise he gets
for loving her, he may well hit her. Therein lies the
problem with many forms of discipline: first, the child
misbehaves because no praise or confidence rewarded
his good behavior; an image as a right-doer has not
been conveyed to him. Second, when he does wrong

he gets attention through punishment. Attention without confidence becomes a drug, unpleasant but *needed* and therefore habit-forming.

Rewards are better than punishments. Rewards give attention and confidence simultaneously. Children are put in the position of being able to win the two things they need most by developing good habits and accomplishing worthwhile things.

Children are remarkably capable human beings. They can do more than we think they can. They can understand more than we think they can. The reason they sometimes don't understand, the actual *cause* of the effect, is that we don't *think* they can.

Five-year-old children can give family home evening lessons. Three-year-olds can be happy for, rather than jealous of, their older sister who gets a birthday invitation. Four-year-olds can have jobs that they *remember* and *do*. Six-year-olds can share others' pain with compassion and concern. All they need is confidence, reinforcement.

Fathers play what is perhaps the key role in the development of children's confidence. Since the child normally sees less of the father than of the mother, the father's approval, signs of love and trust, are all the more important. The father who is committed to being confident in his children, who is looking for praise-worthy things, for gifts, for traits to admire, will, without conscious effort, convey that confidence to his children.

Children are *mirrors* They reflect the confidence that emanates from the parent. The father who has programmed himself to look for and show confidence

will direct toward the child the kind of light that *can*
be reflected and that will steadily and gradually
increase the child's self-esteem.

Sometimes the most obvious ways of showing (and
building) confidence in children are overlooked. The
more direct ways are often best. The *most* direct way
is to tell the child. Sit a three-year-old down, look him
square in the eye, and say, "Son, you are really a fast
runner. You are very good at eating with a fork. You
are good at building things with your blocks. I am
really proud of you."

Try it as an experiment. Think about the specific
things you are proud of about your child. Make a
mental list. Not too long. Just the main things. Think
of the gifts he has, the things (even little ones) that he
does well. Get him alone. Concentrate on him. Tell
him what he's good at. Some children react more than
others (when I do this with my three-year-old he
beams like a sunbeam and is sweetness and light for
twelve hours) but *all* children react. Those who
respond least may be those who need it most.

As a father begins to build confidence and self-
esteem in his child, he begins to see that part of
building is *being sure not to tear down*. Criticism, in
even its subtle forms, can destroy things that have
taken months to build. This is not to say that children
should not be corrected and disciplined. It is *criticism*
that should be avoided. Correction and discipline
show disapproval for something a child has done,
never for the child himself or for his personality or
characteristics. When correction is needed, it should
be given in the spirit of D&C 42:88-92, in *private*,

between the parent and child *alone*, never in front of others or in a humiliating or confidence-robbing way.

The Word-peg "Confidence" — a Summary

A father who is self-programming the concept of "confidence" says to himself:

- ► I *look* for my child's gifts, talents, virtues, sweetness. I *notice* all he does well, all he is, all he is becoming.
- ► I *tell* him! I praise him in every way — by word, look, touch.
- ► I give more *attention* for positive behavior than for negative.
- ► I avoid criticism consciously, carefully. I separate my disfavor with *things he does* from my constant *favor* and confidence in *him*, in who and what he is.
- ► I love my child. I'm more grateful for him than I can express. He is a very important person to me. I am important because I have him! He knows this; he feels it.

2.   Consultantship

The difference between a loving father and a father who is both loving and *wise*, is that the first tries to

give his child all that he wants while the second tries
to give him all that he *needs.*

The second, in his wisdom, gives more opportunities than things, more options than conclusions,
more freedoms than dictates. The first gives the child
a fish. The second gives him a fishing pole.

Our Heavenly Father, whose fathership is perfect
and whose model all fathers should look to, set the
clear example of wisdom. His plan, and that of His
Son, was built around agency and freedom. He rejected
(as did we) the plan of guarantees and managed
supervision, choosing instead the plan of self-
determination and experience, and freedom to ask,
decide, and choose. By committing Himself to agency,
Heavenly Father put Himself in the role of a consultant
rather than a manager. He is a consultant in the
sense that He does not make our decisions or enforce
our directions *and* in the sense that He helps us as we
need Him and ask Him. Perhaps the Lord's greatest
strength is manifest when He lets us make mistakes,
knowing they will hurt us but also knowing it is the
only way for us to grow. Think of His restraint when
He refrains from telling us things before we're ready
for them, from giving us answers before we ask the
questions.

Of course, Heavenly Father gave us earth's agency
only *after* our stay with Him, in His home, but I expect
that even there He let us discover, gave *us* the
privilege of initiative — always stimulating, encouraging, and answering, but rarely demanding,
imposing, or pressing us into a mold.

An interesting study, done by *Life* magazine set
out to explain the differences between two selected

groups of high school students, both of which came from similar homes, income structures, social settings, etc. The first group consisted of well-adjusted kids who were high achievers and *A* students. The second group was composed of students with less self-motivation who made only average grades.

Researchers went back a year at a time, tracing the development of the adolescents in both groups, looking for differences in the home that could explain the differences in school. No clear contrasts showed up until they got back to the pre-school years. There the difference appeared. The difference was the parents. The *A* students had parents who functioned more as consultants than managers. They loved their children but were involved and busy with other things as well. Their general attitude toward their pre-school children was to keep them in a free, stimulating environment; let them explore; respond to their questions; watch for "curious moments" when they could teach their children. The *C* parents were more dominant, more managing. In most cases, they actually spent more time with their children than the *A* parents, but that time consisted of directing the children and force-feeding them with things they were often not interested in. The *C* children had more restricted environments and lived lives that were virtually managed by their parents.

What lesson should fathers learn from the Lord's example and from the *A* and *C* study? Is it to give children absolute freedom? Is it to get busy with other things and let them make their own way? Of course not. It is simply to respect them as persons— to encourage self-discovery, self-determination, self-learning. The lesson is to realize that each personality must unfold in its own unique way; each must learn by a combination of experiences and questions rather than by dictates and too-quick answers. The lesson is that no matter how much we love our children we can't do everything for them. And if we really love them, we won't try. In Elder Neal A. Maxwell's words, "Fathers who do too much for their children will find they can't do much with them."

I recall one particular day that illustrates the contrast between the consulting parent and the managing parent. Linda had a series of Church meetings one Saturday, and I was anxious to spend a whole day alone with the kids. I'd been traveling a lot and perhaps felt guilty for not being with them more. I got up that morning with several things in mind. First, I wanted them to clean up their rooms. Then I wanted to show them how to plant some vegetable seeds in our garden. Finally, I hoped we could all take a bike ride together.

At breakfast I announced my plans. There was the standard complaining about room cleaning. There was general agreement with the garden idea, although Shawni wanted to know why we couldn't go somewhere rather than staying home all day. Then Josh said his bike was broken. To make a long story short, the morning fizzled. The rooms never got clean, I planted by myself the only seeds that got planted, and the kids acted as if I was forcing them to ride their bikes.

A circumstance changed the afternoon. During lunch the phone rang. My secretary reminded me of a press release I had promised to finish by five. I returned to the lunch table and said, "Kids, I've got a little work I have to do. There are some seeds in the shed. The directions are on them, but don't touch them until your rooms are straight. I'll unlock the old clothes chest for costumes if you want to play afterwards. I don't care what you do as long as you clean up. I'll be in the den if you need me."

The afternoon was great. I helped them twice when they had questions about the seeds. All the rooms got cleaned up (I did have to remind Josh twice). I refereed a little disagreement that gave me a chance to teach a principle. (We "backed up" the problem and had the two act out how they could have resolved it without fighting. It was a real teaching moment, because it was related to something that had just happened rather than being a lesson I just happened to want to teach them.) About midafternoon, Shawni announced that they had a show to put on for me. I came out and witnessed their production complete with homemade costumes and curtain calls. Because their show was about a prince and a princess who had babies and families, teaching moments abounded.

By the end of the afternoon my press release was done and I had experienced several positive teaching experiences with the kids on subjects they brought up, subjects relating to what they were doing. I learned that day that children do not need to be told to learn or told what to learn. They need responsive parents. They need a father who is more interested in *them* and in *their* needs and interests of the day than in his own preconceived ideas of what would be fun or what they should learn.

Children are more like plants than like clay. They need to be nourished, not formed; cultivated in their own growth, not pressed into molds.

I want to share with you a simple little document that may be the most valuable aid to fathership I have ever seen. It is a pledge that a close friend once made to himself. He calls it "My Commitment to My Children's Agency." I would probably call it "The Father as Consultant." It reads like this:

1. I will not force my children into my pre-conceived mold of what they should be. I will try to discover who and what they really are as they discover themselves. I will try to expose them to many things and to encourage *their* interests, *their* abilities. (I will not try to make a great ball player out of a natural scientist.)

2. I will try to give them a free and active, open environment. No parts of our house will be off-limits. I will be sure there is an abundance of crafts, projects, books, games, and materials to experiment with.

3. I will *watch* them, listen to them, and answer their questions honestly (with another question whenever I can). I will watch for "teaching moments" and take the time necessary whenever I see one.

4. As much as practical, I will let them make their own decisions. If they know the facts and still make wrong decisions, where the consequences are not too severe I will let those decisions stand and let the children suffer the consequences. Where I must direct them and

make decisions for them, I will explain that Heavenly Father gave me responsibility for them while they are little. Just as He had us in His house before He sent us to earth on our own, so I have them in my house and must teach them right until they are old enough to decide for themselves.

5. I will make my own life as real and full as possible so that I will serve as an example to them of the joy of growing up and becoming an adult. I will show confidence in the gospel and in myself so that they will want to come to me when they have questions or worries.

Because of this "pledge," my friend is a great father. He gives the right priority to his kids without dominating them. He influences them without stifling their initiative. He guides them without pushing them.

When my first son was born, I had some surprisingly strong preconceptions about what kind of boy he would be. I bought him a basketball before he could crawl, a tennis racquet before he could walk. Even as he became old enough to know what they were, he had *no* interest. When I put up a basketball hoop, he was more interested in unscrewing the bolts that held it up than in shooting baskets. When I took him to a basketball game, he watched the scoreboard all evening, fascinated with how the numbers changed and adding up the combined scores. I hate to admit it, but he was about five before I realized he was an amazing boy but in totally different ways than I had first thought I wanted him to be. Since that time, I've followed *his* initiative. We talk about science. We take apart clocks. We play calculator and memory games.

Josh has blossomed. He sees how proud I am of him
in the things he does do well. His stubbornness is
gone. We are extremely close. I am his consultant,
helping him in his fascinating process of self-discovery.

The Savior, of course, was a great consultant. He
guided people in working out their own problems. He
answered questions with questions or with parables.
He made people think, encouraging them to draw their
own conclusions.

Joseph Smith, in one of his most profound and
thought-provoking statements, said, "I teach [the
people] correct principles and they govern themselves." To a surprising degree, this works even with
small children.

As a family, we frequently make a three-hour trip
to Grandma's house. Inevitably little scraps break out
in the rear regions of the station wagon, and Mom
usually looks to Dad as the priesthood power that
should put things right. I guess for years I had been
using the same approach. It consisted of yelling louder
than they did and demanding that they stop fighting.
It never worked very well or for very long.

One day, shortly after I had started programming
myself into the "consultant" role, I tried something
different. I pulled the car to the side of the road and
explained *repentance:* "If you hurt someone in any
way, you should give them a love, say you're sorry,
and ask if they will forgive you." Then Linda and I
demonstrated just how to do this. They watched,
fascinated by this front-seat dramatization. Next I
explained *non-retaliation:* "Jesus said if someone
hurts you or says something mean, don't hurt them

back. Instead love them or say something nice so they'll feel better. Then there won't be a fight. It takes two to fight." Linda and I demonstrated this idea— she hit me, I hugged her.

Then we talked about both principles for a while. I asked the children (ages one to ten) questions and was surprised by how much they understood. Then I said, "This car won't go while there is fighting or yelling going on. It will just stop and wait till someone repents or turns the other cheek."

On the rest of that trip (and on so many since) Linda and I have had our own pleasant conversations, interacting with the kids when they ask questions or when we see something interesting. When the noise level goes up or tempers flare, the car slows down. Usually before it stops someone repents and things quiet down. Then we drive on.

There are two techniques that can be particularly helpful to father-consultants. One is the non-directive conversation method developed by the noted psychiatrist Carl Rogers. "Rogerian technique" consists of letting another person (in this case your child) completely control the direction of your conversation. This is accomplished by simply repeating back, in different words and an interested tone, everything he is saying to you. For example, six-year-old Johnny says, "Dad, Billy hit me on the back today at school."

Dad:	While you were at school Billy hit you?
Johnny:	Yes, and I didn't do anything to him.
Dad:	Billy hit you for no reason because you hadn't done anything to him.

Johnny:	Yes, we were playing ball and we were on the same team and he just hit me.
Dad:	You guys were on the same team and for some reason he got mad and hit you.
Johnny:	Yes, right on the back. I think he thought it was his turn to bat, but it was really mine.
Dad:	Oh, it was your turn but he thought it was his.
Johnny:	Yes, so I had to take the bat from him.
Dad:	So you took the bat from him and he hit you.
Johnny:	Yes, but I hit a double and he batted me in, so we were friends after.
Dad:	Oh, you both played well, so you felt better after.
Johnny:	Yes, and our team won, and I told Billy I was sorry I took the bat.
Dad:	Good, son; I'm proud of you.

Rogerian technique may not always turn out that well, but it will almost always give you a clearer understanding of what your child is really thinking than will a more directive sort of conversation.

The second technique is simpler. I try to have at least once a month a special one-on-one date with each of my children. This is discussed more fully in a later section, but the point to be made here is that *they* decide where we will go and what we will do together. I try to go along, listen, observe — be a consultant rather than a manager.

The Word-peg "Consultantship" —a Summary

A father who is programming himself into being a "consultant" says to his own mind:

- ▶ My children are each unique. Each possesses wonderful gifts that should be recognized and cultivated.
- ▶ They also have minds that are learning and exploring. They are more capable of understanding than I realize.
- ▶ I am a consultant to them. I let them explore, experience, discover. I watch for teaching moments and respond to questions but try not to manage or dictate what they do any more than I have to.
- ▶ I teach them principles and try to be an example of each principle I teach.

3. Calmness-Consistency-Congruence

At first glance, this may seem like a more complex word-peg than the others. It is, however, in some ways the most important of all. A father who can program himself to be *calm* and *consistent* with his children and yet *congruent* (real and honest in his feelings as well as his words), can bring a spirit of peace into his home that helps to make all other principles work just that much better.

Calmness

Doctrine and Covenants section 3 admonishes fathers to "govern their households in meekness." Brigham Young's advice to fathers was to "be mild and sweet to children." Loss of temper and loud voices drive the Holy Ghost from a home. Children, the most accurate of mirrors, quickly pick up the temper pattern and ricochet it throughout a home.

Our little children love to watch "Mr. Rogers" on television. It wasn't until I sat down with them one day that I discovered why. It is because he is so *calm* that it makes them feel calm. Mr. Rogers doesn't do anything very exciting. He just walks around, tells the kids he likes them, appears interested in them, and shows them things—all in a voice so calm, so peaceful that it nearly puts you to sleep. While I was watching Mr. Rogers with our kids, I suddenly remembered a show I used to love as a child for the same basic reason. Remember "Ozzie and Harriet"? A very unexciting show, but one with such subdued feeling. Ozzie could say "Well, now, don't worry; we'll work that out." I used to love the show, and I realize now it was because of the calmness it portrayed.

There are clear links between calmness and security.

Here are four examples of the type of efforts that can develop greater serenity in a home:

1. *A morning devotional.* Ours is very simple, consisting only of a little scripture and our morning prayer. Before the devotional, we have "quiet time," when everyone whispers. The morning starts off on a calm, peaceful note, before the rush begins for breakfast and school.

2. *Classical music.* Most classical music not only awakens children's appreciation (and sometimes their imagination) but also brings a peaceful, calming influence.

3. *A priesthood-dedicated home.* We have dedicated our home with a priesthood prayer. The dedicatory prayer is transcribed and hangs on the wall. It serves as a reminder of a commitment we have all made not to yell in the home. The agreement is, when someone feels he has to yell, whine, or cry, he goes in his own room and closes the door.

4. *Pictures of the Savior.* A family I know has two beautiful Frances Hook wall-pictures of the Savior with small children. The drawings, in pastel chalk, project a warm, calm feeling. We ourselves have a set of video tapes of a film on Christ of which we play a portion each Sunday. Anything connected with the Savior or His words carries a feeling of peace.

A father's ability to be calm around his children relates a lot to his ability to remember what it was like to be a child. If he can be a little analytic, a little removed from the emotion of a moment when a child is screaming, he can combat the outburst not with a retaliation-outburst but with calmness. Often the key is simply to remember how it felt to be a child, how important little things seemed, how easy it was to get upset. Nothing works better in calming down a child than telling him about a time when you felt the same way.

Probably the most important key to calmness is that the father *have* calmness as his conscious goal. Whatever your other objectives for the moment — to teach a family home evening lesson, to get the kids to bed, to have a picnic or climb a mountain with them — try to maintain a second objective which is always the same: "Keep a calm, pleasant spirit whenever you are with them." If this second objective is always in mind, you will not force the family home evening lesson in spite of the chaos all around you, you will not rush the putting-to-bed at the expense of a calm moment together or the joy of really listening to a child's bedtime prayer.

A child's response to calmness is one of the most beautiful rewards a father can have. Children feel calmness and become especially loving in response to it. I have learned to expect that whenever I come into the home feeling calm and peaceful and projecting those feelings to the children, their whole countenance will mirror me. And, inevitably, within ten minutes, one of them comes to me, spontaneously and without even knowing why he's doing it, throws his arms around my neck and says, "I love you, Daddy."

Consistency

Children gain great security from consistency. Erratic behavior, on the other hand, upsets children and makes them insecure.

In our home we have a simple list of things in which we try to be totally consistent:

1. Discipline. (We have a chart of "Family Laws" arrived at together as a family. Each law has a fixed penalty, ranging from going to one's room to a spank. Children can count on consistent, predictable discipline when they violate those laws.)

2. Morning devotional and prayer. (It is usually short, but the children can count on this calm moment each morning.)

3. Responsibility. (Each child has simple responsibilities. We have a "peg board" with a big peg for each child's assignment. He puts the peg in when his daily work is accomplished.)

4. Dinner at six o'clock.

Things that are consistent in a family become traditions. Children gain security and calmness from things that don't change, things they can depend on.

Congruence

A father's behavior must be congruent with his feelings.

It is important that a father's consistency and calmness do not become mechanical or artificial. I know a father who is so artificially calm that his children never know how he feels. I watched him discipline one of them once. His manner was so contrived that it seemed heartless. The child had failed to obey his military-like command, so he picked him up, looked at him and said, "I am not mad at you, Jimmy, and I love you very much but I am now going to spank you." The problem was that he was mad. Jimmy knew it. The father had a right to be mad.

He was bottling it up, putting on a facade of calmness, but I could nearly see (and Jimmy could, too) the steam coming out of his ears.

There is a difference between an uncontrolled temper and righteous indignation. There is also a difference between real calmness and artificially-contained fury.

Christ often taught through righteous indignation. When His apostles made mistakes and should have known better, He reproved them sharply, and they felt His love through His wanting them to be better. Two things distinguished His anger. First, it was always directed at what they did, never at *them*. Second, it was controlled, never out of control. (John tells us that Christ braided a whip before driving the money-changers from the temple.)

It is important to let children see your other emotions as well. I remember when our dog was accidentally poisoned and I couldn't keep my tears back. I didn't want the kids to see me cry, but when Shawni noticed she threw her arms around me and we cried together. Since then, I've never tried to hide any emotion from them.

A father who can program himself into being a combination of *Calmness-Consistency-Congruence* can bring the true Spirit of Christ into his home. His children learn to rely on his consistency and strength. They learn to expect and emulate his calmness, to trust the honesty of his emotions, to know he will be firm and indignant about things that they do wrong.

The essence of simplified fathership is example. You change your children for the better only as you change yourself for the better. Below are two quick illustrations of the importance of example:

1.   We were having a hard time getting the two older girls to practice the violin consistently. After weeks of nagging and pushing, I had a better idea. I got out my old cello and started practicing each morning before breakfast. Within a week, the girls were practicing, too.

2.   Josh's room was always a disaster. I had tried to explain how much better and more peaceful he would feel if he kept it straight, but with no results. One day I brought him into my room, which needed cleaning, and sat him down to watch. While I cleaned, I talked about how nice it would make me feel. I showed him that I enjoyed having it straight. I explained what pride meant and that I was proud of my room. About then, he disappeared. When I finished I peeked into his room. He was cleaning feverishly, with a contented smile on his face.

The Word-peg "Calmness-Consistency-Congruence" —a Summary

A father who is "self-programming" the concept of "Calmness-Consistency-Congruence" says to himself:

► I'm calm in the presence of my children.
  They feel my calmness and respond to it.
► I'm consistent with my children in
  discipline, in being responsive to their
  questions, and in doing certain things they
  can depend on.
► My feelings and behavior with my children
  are congruent. I let them see my real
  emotions, but they are always in control.
  If I get more angry than "righteous
  indignation" would allow, I apologize to
  them.

4. Concentration

It is essential that the father concentrate on each
child as an individual. Children need two kinds of
confidence. One is the security-confidence of being
part of a family institution. The other is the individual-
confidence of liking themselves, of being unique, of
knowing there are certain things they do well. Fathers
can play a major role in this second kind of confidence
simply through the way they *think* about each of their
children. Children need to know that their father
recognizes them as individuals, that they are special to
their dads in ways that the other children *aren't*. Let
me lay out a quick potpourri of ways to avoid treating
children collectively, ways in which to focus on each
child as an individual.

1. *Daddy Dates.* In our family, I set up one special "date" each month with each child. Just the two of us go to a movie or for a hamburger, talking about the child's special interests. My goal is to build his individual confidence. Each child has a "daddy date book" which is nothing more than a note book in which he keeps mementos of each date — a ticket stub or a program. I think they enjoy going through the books and remembering past dates nearly as much as they enjoyed the dates themselves.

2. *Clubs.* Another father has a special "club" with each child. With the eldest daughter, who loves books, he has "The Literary Discussion Group." With his six-year-old son, who is very mechanically minded, he has "The Fixers' Club" (whenever something breaks, the two of them try to fix it together). The clubs not only give each child a special and unique relationship with his dad; they also provide a vehicle for close communication. The father says he learns far more about his boy in their talks while "fixing things" than in any more formal "interview."

3. *Husband-Wife Reviews.* Another father makes a point of taking his wife on a special date once a month during which they confine their discussion to a review of each of the children. They discuss the physical, mental, social, emotional and spiritual progress of each one, his or her unique gifts and needs. Since the wife spends more time with the children, her

thoughts shared are important if she and the
husband are to work together.

4.   *Interviews.* A father who is serving as bishop
     decided that his children needed regular
     "personal priesthood interviews" as much as
     his ward members. Each Sunday he calls
     them into his den one at a time and has them
     report on the past week and tell him their
     goals for the week ahead. A younger man has
     a similar pattern with his little children,
     except that they go into the bathroom because
     it is the only private place in their small
     home. His children call the talks "bathroom
     chats."

5.   *Ten-second Focus* and *Taking Them Along.*
     Another father I want to tell you about says
     he's too busy for any routines such as those
     listed above. He says that whenever he tries a
     "daily program" or a "weekly interview"
     something comes up and he feels guilty for not
     following it. His method, therefore, for giving
     his children individual attention is quite
     different. First, no matter how busy he is, he
     finds at least one moment a day (sometimes
     only a few seconds) to interact directly with
     each child. He focuses *all* his attention on that
     child, perhaps for just one question: "How did
     that math test go? Good — I'm proud of you,
     Jim." This is enough for Jim to know he
     cares, that dad's aware of something specific
     about Jim. Second, this father takes one of
     his children with him whenever it is possible.
     Sometimes the outing is as brief as an errand,
     sometimes as long as an overnight business

trip. The travel turns into private, one-on-one interaction. The father tries to ask and listen more than he talks.

The more children a father has, the more difficult it is to give each one individual attention. This can be compounded by the fact that, in larger families, each child has more need to be singled out for special attention. One help in a large family is for the father to make a point of privately telling each child how important his individual place in the family is. "You are the oldest and your example means so much to the others." "You are our youngest daughter and we'll always have a special love for you." "You're our blondie."

Some time ago, Linda and I were worried about two of our middle children who seemed to be getting less attention and recognition than the others. We set up a family home evening with three games designed to teach each of the children about his unique importance. The first game involved standing each child up, one at a time, on a stool while each of the other family members related something he liked about that child. The next game was to sit in a circle and take turns saying, "I can't _____, right now, but I can _____ ." (We knew we were getting somewhere when the middle girl said, "I can't play the violin like Saren yet, but I can *really* do cartwheels.") We clapped for each other. The game held our interest for a surprisingly long time. The third game involved making a large chart called "The Family Experts' Board." On it we listed each person in the family and the things at which they were especially expert. The baby was the family expert at loud noises. One daughter was the expert at ballet and cooking; another was the expert story-teller and the best flute player. The little four-year-old said he was an expert at putting on Band-Aids.

By the time the evening was over, we felt that each child had a clearer view of who he was and why he had individual worth.

Some of the ideas and methods listed above may be directly appealing to you as a father; others may not. Keep in mind that the ideas are only *examples* of a *principle*. It is the principle, the concept, the word-peg, that needs to be understood and programmed into your inner mind. Once the principle is there — once you realize how important it is not to treat your children *collectively* — your own mind, without much effort, will find its own ways to build children's individual egos. You will be able to develop personal relationships with them in a natural and free way and, in a broader sense, to cultivate within *yourself* each of the four fathership qualities we have been discussing.

One grand way of giving individual time and instilling confidence in a child is to *teach* him something. Linda and I have rejected the traditional saying that a stranger can teach our children better than we can. Linda teaches music lessons to each child every day. I give them a tennis lesson each week. Perhaps more valuable than the music and tennis they learn, are the things *we* learn about each of them as we teach them. Then there is confidence we can build *into* each of them and the individual relationships we build *with* each of them.

As you begin to feel that you know the unique strengths and gifts of a particular child, it is a good exercise to write out a description of that child which includes each gift. The writing helps you focus real attention on that child. (The reading, out loud *to* the child, improves his confidence both in himself and in your love for and interest in him.)

Perhaps the best way to learn how to treat a child as an individual is to pray about each one, to ask the Lord to reveal to you their strengths and to tell you how to communicate fully and individually with each one.

The Word-peg ''Concentration'' — a Summary

A father who is self-programming the concept of ''Concentration'' says to himself:

- ▶ Each of my children is unique. I appreciate separate things about each of them.
- ▶ I find ways to be with each one alone and to talk to each one alone. I realize that each may need a different kind of communication with me.
- ▶ I look for the unique gifts that each one has and compliment it and cultivate it.

How Do I Become These Qualities?

An incident which occurred several years ago led to the idea of the "self-programming" method for improving fathership.

I passed George one day while I was jogging. He was jogging in the other direction. I said "Hi," but he didn't notice me or hear me. It looked as if he was talking to himself. His lips were moving. The second time around the block, we met again. He *was* talking to himself.

"Hellooo, George," I said — loudly.

His eyes glanced up as we passed. "Morning," he said, still hardly seeing me.

The third time I stopped him. "George, what are you doing, building bridges while you run?" (George was a structural engineer.)

George looked at me, up out of the corners of his eyes (George was five-foot-four inches.) He was trying to decide whether to tell me. After squinting at me for a moment he said, "Run the other way around the block with me and I'll explain."

George liked to answer questions with questions. He said, "Why do you run?"

I said, "To stay in shape, to live longer, to enjoy the fresh air."

He said, "Mmmmmm, me too, but those are all secondary reasons for me. I jog to program my sub-conscious mind."

"To do what, George?"

"To self-program. What's happening while I jog is that I'm becoming a better person. I'm improving the way I relate to other people and I'm making myself mentally stronger and more spontaneous."

It didn't seem so at the time — but what George said that morning made eminent sense. He *was* becoming a better person while he jogged. He *was* programming his subconscious mind.

What George continued to tell me, between breaths as we jogged together, was this: "Most people spend all their time trying to change things outside of themselves. They are working for a new car, a new TV. They are trying to change their jobs, to raise their salaries. They are trying to change their wives or their children. Often they are well-meaning. They want to change something for the better — prepare their Primary lesson so they can change the kids they teach, and so on."

George glanced over to see if I was listening. I was. He went on:

"I think the thing we should be working on is ourselves. The thing we ought to be trying to change is us— the inside. That's what Christ did. He spent His first thirty years working on who He was, becoming perfect enough within Himself to change everyone who would ever live through His own perfection and example. The only real way to change other people or things is to change yourself. If you want to be a better father, you don't change your kids; you change yourself. If you want to do better at your job, you don't change your work; you change yourself. If you want to help the kids in the class you teach, you change yourself into a better teacher and a better example."

I'd run further now than I normally did (George was more of a distance man than I was), but I stayed with him because I was fascinated. "That's very interesting, George, but what are you doing to change yourself while you are running?" George was excited now. He was huffing and puffing but his voice had the tone of a Columbus telling about his discovery of a new world.

"Doctors tell us—psychiatrists, too—that exercise not only opens up the heart and the circulation, it opens up the mind, clears the cobwebs, makes the brain more receptive to ideas, to what I call *self-programming.*"

"What do you mean by that, George?"

"Well, you see, the subconscious mind is programmed by the input it receives. When I fail at something, my subconscious gets a message that I can't do it. When I hook the golf ball with my driver, my subconscious gets the message that I can't hit straight. When I succeed at something, my subconscious gets a positive bit of programming. We are all our own creators, in a way. What we do and think makes us what we are."

"Yes, but what about the running, George?"

"I'm getting to that. You see, the interesting thing about the subconscious is that it can't tell the difference between something that happens and something that is *thought*. And it can't tell the difference between something someone else says to it and something *you* say to it. So, I tell myself, while I'm running: "I am a spontaneous person. I notice unexpected beauty and unplanned opportunities." Then I think about *evidence* of this: how I noticed the clouds between the mountains last week, the surprise I found for my wife at the auction. My subconscious believes it. I become more what I want myself to be."

I liked what George was saying, liked it enough that I began to try it myself. My own major priorities were my wife and my children. I decided I would quit trying so hard to change them and instead use George's method to change myself—to change my husbandship and fathership.

It was an interesting process. I identified some areas that I felt I needed to improve on, then refined them into a small number of *qualities* that I wanted to obtain. For the first little while, as I jogged, I simply thought about each quality for a moment and tried to imagine the setting and circumstances in which I could apply it. As time went by, I was able to think of, while I ran, occasions when I *had* applied those qualities. Thus I was able to start saying to myself, "I *am* a calm father. I *have* a quality of calmness when I am around my children that they can feel, that makes them feel calm. Yesterday when I came home I handled Josh and Saydi's fight with calmness."

I soon became aware that I was exhibiting some of the qualities subconsciously, without thinking about them. I found that I was more aware of the children and of the teaching moments that presented themselves. I was, by then, doing less planning of specific activities and time with the children but was actually spending more time with them. And it felt less of a burden. I seemed to react instinctively with the answer or example they needed.

The pattern I suggest to you is a simple one. While running (or while shaving, if you prefer) program yourself as a father by saying to yourself, "I am confident in my children. I have confidence in them. I show confidence in them." Then hold your mind on that subject and let it do its own search for things you have recently done that showed confidence and for coming opportunities to show confidence. Then go on. "I am a consultant to my children. I try to leave much freedom, decision, and initiative to them. I respond to their questions, etc." Then send your mind on a backward and forward search for that quality. Next, go on to Calmness-Consistency-Congruence, then to Concentration.

At the beginning do it every day. (It only takes five or ten minutes once you are used to it.) Later, after the qualities are established in you, two or three times a week is enough to keep you active and improving.

The subconscious mind is *programmable*. It will cause you to become what you tell it you are. Because of its special powers, we *can* become better fathers, not by changing our children but by changing ourselves.